NO-DEFAULT LIVING

LIVING

Pursuing God's Great Dream
For Your Life

by Jim Gordon

Scripture quotations are from:

New Living Translation®, copyright ©1996, 2004, 2007. Used by permission of Tyndale House Publishers, Inc., Carol Stream, Illinois 60188.

New King James Version®, ©1979, 1980, 1982 by Thomas Nelson, Inc. Used by permission. All rights reserved.

King James Version, The Authorized (King James) Version. Rights in the Authorized Version in the United Kingdom are vested in the Crown. Reproduced by the permission of the Crown's patentee, Cambridge University Press.

Holman Christian Standard Bible®, copyright ©1999, 2000, 2002, 2003, 2009 by Holman Bible Publishers, used by permission.

New International Version®, copyright ©1973, 1978, 1984 by the International Bible Society. Used by permission of Zondervan. All rights reserved worldwide.

New American Standard Bible®, copyright ©1960, 1962, 1968, 1971, 1972, 1973, 1975, 1977, 1995 by the Lockman Foundation. Used by permission. All rights reserved.

The English Standard Version® Bible, copyright ©2001 by Crossway, a publishing ministry of Good News Publishers. Used by permission. All rights reserved.

This book is dedicated to the children Jesus gifted us with:

Elizabeth

Joshua

Trevor

Nathan

Jeremy

Michael

Jeffrey

Caleb

Christel

The apostle John said it best thousands of years ago: *"I have no greater joy than to see that my children walk in truth"* (3 John 1:4).

I am so honoured to be your Dad!

CONTENTS

Preface

This book is the fruit of reflection on many years of being too busy and not intentional enough. I would much rather have been able to write a book telling people, "Hey! Live your life in exactly the same way I lived mine!" Unfortunately, *No-Default Living* is not like that; on the contrary, this book encourages the reader to do what I failed to do for many years—live a deliberate, no-default kind of life that ultimately leads to the authentic significance and impact that Jesus promised (John 10:10).

Most people go with the flow, take the easy road, or pursue the path of least resistance.

Look around you! The world needs leaders more than ever before—so live a no-default life and lead the way! You'll be surprised how many will follow...

Introduction to
No-Default Living

Most people today live by default.

Now, you won't find the term "no-default living" in the Bible, but you will find Jesus' description of no-default living when He speaks of "abundant life."

> The thief comes to rob, and steal, and to destroy. But I have come that you might have abundant life (John 10:10[1]).

How do you define abundant life? Actually, an abundant life may look differently on the outside for

---

1   Unless otherwise noted all quotations are from the New Living Translation.

1

each one of us: it's an inner thing! This abundance, however, is experienced as each of us thoughtfully applies our faith to all areas of our lives. In so doing, we learn to trust Jesus in every facet of life!

Abundant life is much less of an external checklist that we need to complete.
- ✓ fancy car
- ✓ nice clothes
- ✓ beautiful home and family
- ✓ successful career
- ✓ etc.

No, it is a recipe for life. Abundant living is choosing to be engaged in the present, experiencing the moment, living with purpose through the choices I make as I pursue God's great dream for my life!

Abundant living occurs where choices have been made in every area to trust Jesus and to define exactly what trusting Jesus looks like. It's about bringing real, genuine faith into our decision-making choices. Abundant, no-default living is the result of methodically asking the question "How can my experience in this area of my life most glorify Jesus?" Now the answer you come up with may or may not be a perfect picture, but it will be an excellent starting place, and will bring a helpful perspective adjustment.

On the flip side, default settings are preset choices made without consulting you.

On your computer, for example, the default settings are the probable choices and preferences that most people would select when using their computer. Actually, default settings save you a lot of time and bother! If we all had to choose every setting, and make a decision about every possible, available choice before we could use our computer, it could take days to get started.

Imagine choosing from all possible fonts and sizes, colours and configurations, numerical display preferences, the formatting options for paragraphs, sentences, bullets, numbering, and cases. Getting started would take a very long time indeed! And on and on it goes! Literally thousands of choices would have to be made! Now, with default settings, the choices are still available, but in the absence of a decision to change, a choice has already been made for us!

The font style for this book you are reading is called Helvetica; however, when I started typing for the first time on my computer, the default setting was Times New Roman. I didn't choose it—the font style of Times New Roman was chosen for me. It was by default.

Without my decision to change, you'd be reading text that looks like this!

Now, default settings in the context of computer documents may well produce a document that is reasonably okay, but it won't be an accurate representation of your creative signature, flair, personality, etc... Creative flair is a result of looking at the options and personalizing the document to represent who you are.

Now, this analogy shouldn't be pulled too tightly. The reality is that sometimes life happens, and we suffer the results of other people's choices. Default living, though, is an abdication of responsibility. It's abdication of personal choices. Life just happens, and others make choices for you. You abdicate responsibility for things, and take on a victim mentality.

In reality, many people live their lives by default and have reasonably successful lives. However, they've robbed themselves of the chance to make choices to believe and trust in Christ.

You're not trusting Jesus when you live by default. Faith is a choice, and you're not living by faith if you're not making a choice.

In reflection, some of my life has been lived by default. I'm sad to say it, but it's true. Some choices I didn't make because I didn't understand that a choice was even available! (What?! There's a font type other than Times New Roman?!)

"The secret of living a life of excellence is merely a matter of thinking thoughts of excellence. Really, it's a matter of programming our minds with the kind of information that will set us free."

- Chuck Swindoll [2]

---

2   Charles R. Swindoll, *Dear Graduate: Letters of Wisdom from Charles R. Swindoll* Nashville, Tennessee: Thomas Nelson Inc., 2007.

Other choices I put off because I was immature and didn't see the value of making them. Still others, I neglected because I was afraid to face the truth that was necessary to make the decision or was afraid of failure.

Let me use a personal example:

For many years, I simply assumed the Lord would take care of my family's finances, and it didn't matter what I was being paid. God would provide. My assumption was (and still is) actually true! What was missing from my life, though, was an accompanying decision to more rigorously approach our finances, and develop a financial plan for our future. I could have—but I didn't. Instead, I chose to live by default—assuming it would all work out in the end. In other words, my original motivation was faith in God but it was clouded with presumption. Presumption says "God will take care of it, so I don't have to get involved with reconciling the details."

Hope alone is not a plan.

Think of Moses, leader of the children of Israel, as he watched Pharoah's army approach, pinning the Israelites followers between the Egyptian army and the Red Sea. Moses said to them *"Stand still, and see the salvation of God"* (Exodus 14:13). Almost immediately, God responded to Moses. *"Why are you standing still? Stretch out your rod and walk through on dry land!"* God gives each of us an intimate, critical role to play in our own deliverance. Sometimes we want to stand still and 'let God take care of it'. But He says, stretch out your rod and walk through.

No Default, No Regret

Assuming things will just work out falls short of faith and trust in God—it is living *by default.* Faith requires an actual decision that embarks us on a deliberate course of action. God honours faith! Without a real engagement of my faith, I don't make deliberate choices. I go with the flow and presume it will be okay in the end. My choices are by default. Inevitably, default living produces regrets; no-default living produces no regrets!

I've come to discover, though, that even in the middle of my regret, there is still hope! If the pain of regret stimulates us toward change and no-default living, then we have the opportunity to turn our regrets into spiritual energy—divine motivation to live life God's way! This is exactly what happened to the Apostle Paul! Listen as he writes,

> *For I am the least of all the apostles, unworthy to be called an apostle, because I persecuted the church of God. But by God's grace I am what I am, and His grace toward me was not ineffective. However, I*

worked more than any of them, yet not I,
but God's grace that was with me.
(I Corinthians 15:9-10 HCSB[3])

Reading between the lines, we can sense that
Paul very well may have been immobilized by
regret. After all, he was personally responsible for
the imprisonment and death of Christians prior to
his conversion.

I persecuted the followers of this Way to
their death, arresting both men and women
and throwing them into prison, as also the
high priest and all the Council can testify. I
even obtained letters from them to their
brothers in Damascus, and went there to
bring these people as prisoners to
Jerusalem to be punished.
(Acts 22:4,5 NIV[4])

Self-examination will always produce regret.

Regret is a circular thought pattern: *"If only I hadn't
done that, I wouldn't be where I am, I'm so sorry I
did that. If only I hadn't done that, I wouldn't be
where I am."* This is the circle of regret.

---

3   Holman Christian Standard Bible

4   New International Version

We break the circle of regret with trust in Jesus' promise: all things work together for good and God can and will use where I am today for good - my good, my family's good, and the world's good. We must turn regret into motivation through the application of grace.

Paul is a great example of this! He turned regret over his past into motivation to live for Christ! In the end, the grace of God energized him more than anything else!

Your story is hopefully not as dramatic as Paul's, but the process of God's grace can work the same in you!

Wrong thinking that produces wrong actions avoids examination and resists inviting Christ in. The active ingredient necessary to transition from regret to no-default living is grace.

Rather than being immobilized by your regrets for the past, God's grace can help you change to no-default living.

Then, intentionally, you can help others who are presently living the default lifestyle you once lived! Tell your story in order to help others!

"The bridge of grace will bear your weight, brother. Thousands of big sinners have gone across that bridge, yea, tens of thousands have gone over it. Some have been the chief of sinners and some have come at the very last of their days but the arch has never yielded beneath their weight. I will go with them trusting to the same support. It will bear me over as it has for them."

– Charles Spurgeon [5]

---

5   Iain Murray, *The Forgotten Spurgeon*. Carlisle, Pennsylvania: Banner of Truth, 2009.

What Can You Do Right Now To Start No-Default Living?

✓ Invest time reflecting on your life. On the next page, list five areas and/or incidents where you "go with the flow" instead of making active choices.

✓ List five choices others have made for you that you should have made yourself. Ask yourself the question, "Is it time that I make my own choice?" Note: that doesn't mean your choice will be different, it may be the same choice—but now it's yours!

✓ Repeat this short declaration out loud: "Thank you, Jesus, for the abundant life you have for me. Help me to make the choices in my life that lead me to experiencing that abundance."

✓ Use the Notes and Next Steps page to journal.

Notes and Next Steps

_____

_____

_____

_____

_____

_____

_____

_____

_____

_____

_____

_____

_____

Your Identity

Chapter One

Ever since the garden when God said to Adam, *"Where are you?"* (Genesis 3:9 HCSB), the Lord has wanted us to understand we are lost without Him! Our sense of "lost-ness" is not geographical in nature; it's personal, and it affects every aspect of our being. As a result, each of us is searching for meaning, for significance, for identity.

The Default Setting: Absence of Identity

When we question our identity, and do not fully recognize who we are in Christ, we become prey for the devil and fall into the traps hidden within our culture. Consequently, we look for identification in other places and with other people. We may allow ourselves to be labeled with others in an attempt to establish our own identity. We might gravitate to and align ourselves with some group, and participate in the group dynamic that provides us with a sense of identity security. It's easier to share in the identity of the group (usually defined by exterior criteria like style of dress, way of talking, common experiences, expectations, being perceived as being the same) than do the hard work of discovering our own identity.

This begs the question 'why' - and ultimately - "who will love me?" This question becomes the basis of performance-based living. In that mindset, the things I do, how I dress, who I associate with, the words I use are all driven by the desire to be loved and accepted: a never-ending quest to prove ourselves worthy of love.

Such a mindset cripples our identity. It assumes since we do not feel loved, we are not loved. Therefore, we lack something and are incomplete. As long as this mental structure is driving your actions you WILL have an identity crisis. As long as I live this way, I will never discover my true identity.

Personally, one of the lowest points in my life resulted from my own insecurity—because I wasn't yet established in my true identity in Christ.

I had just been officially recognized as the one who would become the next senior pastor of our church. A person I respected, and whose opinion I valued, came to me and said, "I don't think you're the one to lead this church." I was devastated—and it all came from my identity issues. I wrestled with myself, with my calling, with my weaknesses, and with my inabilities. Those deep waters were so painful, and yet, so necessary. God uses difficult times so we might resolve the identity issue!

As I look back, I clearly understand the dynamics in play; I am grateful, by God's grace, I eventually climbed up out of the emotional hole I was in—those days were the darkest days of depression and wrestling with God I have ever had. They were also the beginning of a much longer process to establish truth in my heart and mind that has proven to be an anchor for my soul. I am who I am by God's grace; He has called me and established me with a specific mission in mind. I am in Christ!

Identity Theft

Jesus says either you trust in Him and have abundant life, or you are being robbed; there is no middle ground:

> *The thief comes to rob, and steal, and to destroy. But I have come that you might have abundant life (John 10:10).*

The devil is actively working to steal your identity and give you a cheap, false imitation! The adversary of your soul would like nothing better than to take from you the good things God has given you, to steal from you the bright future the Lord has provided, and to destroy every wonderful aspect of your life. He starts this process of robbery by attempting to steal away from you the truth of who you are. When there is confusion about your identity, then your God-given destiny is in jeopardy. Let this book be an encouragement for you to pursue the identity God has given you!

This concept of identity is an issue that must be settled in our hearts and minds before God can fully have His way in our lives! The day we fully understand who we are in Jesus Christ, is the day our lives will change forever! Don't let the devil rob you of your identity!

No-Default Living: An Identity Immersed In Christ

Understanding that our identity emanates from our relationship with Jesus comes through revelation. It comes by the Holy Spirit teaching us, rather than by drawing strictly academic conclusions.

> *Since you have been raised to new life with Christ, set your sights on the realities of Heaven, where Christ sits on God's right hand in the place of honour and power. Let heaven fill your thoughts. Do not think only about things down here on earth. For you*

died when Christ died, and your real life is hidden with Christ in God.
(Colossians 3:1-3)

Without this revelation that our life is in Christ, we will automatically attempt to establish our own identity. There will be a perpetual, inward fight to prove our worth, our identity. Many people have struggled with this fight for identity all their lives. Sadly, many have gone to their graves not fully knowing who they are, or who God destined them to be.

With identity issues unresolved, there will be problems stemming from deep insecurities that arise in many forms and fashions. Unreal expectations, no tolerance for mistakes, inability to take criticism, a persecution complex, or an unhealthy fixation with being right can all be indicators of insecurities based on identity issues.

Identity Confirmed in Baptism

When we understand its significance, baptism can settle the identity issue forever! Unfortunately, many of us never fully realize what baptism has done for us. Through our conversion and water baptism we make declarations. We died with Christ; we are immersed into Christ; we are raised with Christ. More than anywhere else, it is in water baptism that we declare by our actions that we are in Christ! *"For as many of you as have been baptized into Christ have put on Christ"* (Galatians 3:27 KJV[6]).

Romans 10:9-10 states:

> *If you confess with your mouth Jesus as Lord, and believe in your heart that God raised Him from the dead, you will be saved. For with the heart a person believes, resulting in righteousness, and with the mouth he confesses, resulting in salvation. (NAS[7])*

This Scripture says that with our heart we believe, and with our mouth we confess. Confession is taking a spiritual reality and declaring it into existence. With both actions and words we activate and engage our faith.

Later, in 2 Corinthians 4:18, Paul tells us that *"things which are seen are temporal, things which are not seen are eternal"* (NAS). Gregory and Stone, authors of *The Rest of the Gospel*, give excellent insight into this idea by using the metaphor of a line separating the seen from the unseen. Consider the unseen as being above the line, and the seen and temporal world being below

---

6   King James Version

7   New American Standard

the line. Eternal always trumps temporal. What is unseen always trumps what is seen.

God declares believers in Jesus as *"totally righteous"* (2 Corinthians 5:20). That is true above the line. However, in my observation and experience below the line I may see myself as very unrighteous. Our true identity is always found above the line. What is true above the line changes the behaviour of what is below the line.

Identity as an Extension of Performance

As long as you are living by default and defining your identity by your below-the-line performance, you will experience failure. When you live a no-default life you know what is above the line and it changes what you do and how you act below the line. Prime examples of this? Baptism, and praying the Lord's Prayer.

Romans 6 explains in detail what happens when we are baptized. It is in this chapter we recognize that what we see below the line (what is temporary) doesn't always match up with what is above the line (what is eternal). *"And since we died with Christ, we know we will also live with him"* (Romans 6:8). I died with Christ. Did I experience that below the line? No. Is it true above the line? Through Christ, Yes!

"So you also should consider yourselves to be dead to the power of sin and alive to God through Christ Jesus" (Romans 6:11). I am dead to sin, and alive to God. Did I experience that below the line? No. Is it true above the line? Through Christ, Yes!

So, in baptism, we are immersed into Christ and obtain a new identity that is inextricably woven with the person of Christ! We are in Him, and He is in us! We may not understand it fully, and at times it may not seem reasonable, because what we see, hear and feel is temporary; it's below the line. But that doesn't change what is eternally true, it doesn't change what is above the line.

By engaging our faith, we declare and proclaim the eternal 'above the line' truth that we are dead to sin and alive to God. As we do, a new type of experience enlightens us—it is *revelation!* An understanding that I am in Christ becomes real to me and confirms to me that I am Christ's! As the old hymn says,

> *Closer to God, closer I cannot be,*
> *For in the person of His Son, I am as close as He!*
> *Dearer to God, dearer I cannot be,*
> *For in the person of His Son, I am as dear as He!*

Identity: Does it Come From Birth or Performance?

It seems within our Western culture we are obsessed with productivity to the point that it defines our identity. As a result, we often wrestle with identity issues because we believe we have to *succeed* in our career, in our ministry, and in our work—all to confirm our worth. But this is backwards! Our worth is based on our identity in Christ, not on our performance!

The prevalent misunderstanding of identity in Western thinking is rooted in ancient philosophy. The ancient Greek mindset has become the basis of present Western thought. In this perspective, failure is seen as the pathway to disqualification. Is it any wonder we have a generation of people who have experienced failure, and are now searching for meaning and significance?

The Hebrew worldview on the other hand, viewed failure as the pathway to experience and maturity. An established identity in Christ is the only lasting antidote to Western thought's perpetual side-effects of stress, low self-esteem, fear of failure, perfectionism, workaholism, and any and all other performance-based issues.

When we are rooted in our true, above-the-line identity in Christ, the internal, cramping pressure to always perform, to always look good, to always do things just the right way dissolves into nothing, completely losing its hold on us. Within that new-found freedom, we discover a new, vibrant, and healthy drive to pursue Christ and operate out of grace.

Jesus' Identity

At Jesus' baptism, the Heavenly Father settled Jesus' identity forever, when He said from Heaven, *"This is My Beloved Son, in whom I am well pleased"* (Matthew 3:17 KJV).

The three elements of this statement:

- He is My Son (relationship)
- He is Beloved (unconditional love)
- I am pleased with Him (affirmation)

...all had a bearing on settling and confirming Jesus' identity.

In the same way:

- The Lord has established relationship by making us His children: *"Behold what manner of love the Father has bestowed upon us, that we should be called the children of God"* (I John 3:1 NKJV[8]).

---

8   New King James Version

- He has confirmed His unconditional love for us: *"God proves His own love for us in that, while we were still sinners, Christ died for us"* (Romans 5:8 HCSB).

- And He has affirmed us, by choosing us in Christ: *"For He chose us in Him, before the foundation of the world"* (Ephesians 1:4 HCSB).

What Can You Do Right Now To Start Redefining Your Identity?

✓ If you're not baptized (immersed in water) as a believer, then make plans to do it! Jesus and the apostles commanded us— and in so doing you are identifying with Christ! (see Matthew 28:18-20; Acts 2:38)

✓ Start to discover from the Bible—and then speak out loud—who you are in Christ! Begin this process by committing to memory the verse: *"I am crucified with Christ, nevertheless, I live: yet not I, but Christ lives in me. And the life which I now live in the flesh I live by the faith of the Son of God, who loved me, and gave Himself for me."* (Galatians 2:20 NKJV)

✓ On the desktop of your computer, develop a file: *My Daily Confessions*. Include statements that are declarations of who you are in Christ.

For example:

- *I am loved by God*

- *I have Jesus living in me*

- *I am a son of God living a victorious and abundant life*

Read these statements out loud every morning.

Notes and Next Steps

_____

_____

_____

_____

_____

_____

_____

_____

_____

_____

_____

_____

_____

_____

Your Life's
Purpose and Calling

Chapter Two

Gary Barkalow, in his book *It's Your Call*, says that everyone has a calling on their life, a specific impact they're meant to have.

God is calling each one of us to a specific, personal purpose and destiny. He has a life course that is custom-made, tailored for you and for me. God has a destined assignment and unique activities for you and I to engage in.

Since the Lord knew what He wanted us to do before we were born, He equipped us with gifts, talents, passions and aptitudes that would fit with our assignment. When we are born, He calls us to a life and purpose prepared for us.

> *For you are saved by grace through faith, and this is not from yourselves; it is God's gift—not from works, so that no one can boast. For we are His creation, created in Christ Jesus for good works, which God prepared ahead of time so that we should walk in them. (Ephesians 2:8-10 HCSB)*

Our calling is directly related to good works the Lord has for us to do and the impact He wants us to have on the world. The key to applying this without slipping into performance or works-based living is the *context* within which our good works take place: grace. His grace gives us the ability to create results that far exceed our effort.

Try this analogy: good works done from a performance-based context could be compared to hammering a bucket of nails into a length of lumber manually, with a hammer.

Good works done from a place of grace require much less effort and striving. It's as though you are given a nail gun for building homes that can drive hundreds of nails in an incredibly short time.

When we are moving in our calling, in the context of grace, the impact we have is often disproportionate to our effort.

The above verses indicate we are saved only by faith; yet, they also explain there are good works the Lord has destined or called us to fulfill. As much as God has "good works" and plans for individuals, there's a similar universal calling He has placed on all of our lives:

- We have all been given gifts, passions, and aptitudes.

- He has placed inside all of us a desire to be used by God, not because of identity issues that drive us to seek approval and validate our worth, but rather, motivated by a desire to give Jesus glory.

- There are good works He has waiting for all of us to do. We are exhorted to *"make our calling and election sure"* (2 Peter 1:10 NKJV). We confirm what God has done by moving into it and operating in the accompanying gifts, passions, and aptitudes.

Paul was called to be a messenger from God, as we read in Galatians 1:15, *"God, who from my birth set me apart and called me by His grace, was pleased to reveal His Son in me"* (HCSB).

The work we allow God to do inside of us develops character. There are those who fail in their calling because their outward success - resulting from their natural gifts and talents - can't be properly sustained by their inner character. The perfect character qualities of Galatians 5 (the fruit of the Spirit) are evident in those whom Jesus lives through - those with healthy identities. Character is a result of the Spirit living within us.

Specifically, the good works God created ahead of time for the Apostle Paul to do was preaching the Gospel to the Gentiles (non-Jewish people).

The calling on people's lives involves things the Lord wants them to do: and that is a function of their outer life, their visible life. More important than what they do, however, is who they are - their identity. Again, it is no surprise to acknowledge a person's calling is impacted most by their sense of identity, a key component of their inner life.

As long as there is a discrepancy between our outer life and inner life, our calling will be crippled. The gifts we have been given to fulfill our personal mandate may take us to places of achievement and recognition, but without the personal strength of our private life, we are destined for failure. Gifts and talent alone may take us to the heights; only our character can keep us there!

Consider Jesus' parable of the house built on a rock, and the house built on the sand found in Matthew 7:24-27:

Anyone who listens to my teaching and follows it is wise, like a person who builds a house on solid rock.

Though the rain comes in torrents and the floodwaters rise and the winds beat against that house, it won't collapse because it is built on bedrock.

But anyone who hears my teaching and doesn't obey it is foolish, like a person who builds a house on sand. When the rains and floods come and the winds beat against that house, it will collapse with a mighty crash.

This was spoken in reference to those who acted on His words, and those who didn't. The parable, though, is illustrative in other ways as well. The Lord demonstrated *that which was hidden beneath the surface* was more important than that which was visible above.

Confirmation

Our calling needs to be confirmed by others and by the church. This process may be slow and difficult, but necessary since God has wired us to be interdependent parts of the body of Christ, the church. We must not be lone rangers out doing our own thing; we are to serve the church and others through our calling.

Our culture values independence. Which means it's a rarity to find Christians who want to be true disciples, learners, and are willing to submit to God-ordained authority and say, "Speak into my life, show me the way!" This lack of submission results in a calling being short-circuited, or rendered ineffective by the devil's temptations to pride, self-reliance, and independence.

The Ultimate Goal of Our Calling

Romans 8:29 declares: *"For those He foreknew, He also predestined to be conformed to the image of His Son, so that He would be the firstborn among many brothers"* (HCSB).

Ultimately, our destiny is to be made like Jesus! We are to be transformed into His image. This is our universal, general, but definitive calling in life. In fact, as we study the life of Jesus Himself, there are things for us to learn.

He said in John 18:37, *"I was born for this, and I have come into the world for this: to testify to the truth"* (HCSB). Luke 19:10 reads, *"For the Son of Man came to seek and to save the lost"* (ESV[9]) and Matthew 20:28, *"The Son of Man came not to be served, but to serve, and to give His life—a ransom for many"* (HCSB). Jesus knew His calling.

---

9   English Standard Version

If you don't yet know the details of the specific calling God has on your life, you do know the general calling He has for you—to become more like Jesus in character, to love and accept others.

Pursue this part of your calling in every way you can, and you'll be surprised how Jesus will lead you into specifics for your life.

Reaching Our Calling

Along the Christian journey, traveling from point A to point B never seems to be a straight line! You may be convinced that you're meant to have a certain impact or are called to some purpose, yet find the perceived pathway to take you there almost impossible! What you must remember is that your calling is first, a person you become, and second, a destination you reach. Calling starts with preparation; it's *becoming* first, and *doing* after.

"I want to play a role in eradicating global hunger." This sense of calling is certainly noble. However, the impact starts with cultivating a heart of compassion for those who suffer in your immediate sphere of influence. Acquiring the education, credentials, or platform for larger impact are also important, but they will be an outflow or consequence of who you become.

The life lessons needed to prepare us for our calling are often filled with convoluted turns and twists. However, one thing remains straight and constant—the Lord's vision and purpose for all His children is to build the character of Christ into us!

Regardless of your perceived distance away from your goal or ministry, settle one thing in your mind: *you* are the ministry! The fulfillment of your calling has more to do with who you are than what you have done! Put the emphasis on being rather than doing; your personal development of faith, ministry, and gifting is critical.

"Next to faith this is the highest art - to be content with the calling in which God has placed you."

-Martin Luther [10]

10   Luther, Martin. *Martin Luther's Christmas Book*. Roland H. Bainton ed. Augsburg Books, 1948.

What Can You Do Right Now To Start to Confirm Your Calling?

✓ Establish a personal development plan: your calling is based on who you are, so start reading books that will build you up— even if the information doesn't directly apply to your situation right now! Leadership books, spiritual teaching, and books that enhance your character can be included. On the Notes and Next Steps page, list five activities to include in your personal development plan (titles of books to read, podcasts to listen to, names of leaders to mentor you, leadership events to attend, etc.)

✓ Do you know what your gifts are? Find someone to help you identify them! Your calling will be related to the gifts God has given you!

✓ Your calling begins with who you are. Eventually it will include what you do. Identify the skills you will need in order to fulfill your calling. Develop a plan to increase those skills in your life.

Notes and Next Steps

Responsibility vs. Self-Reliance

Chapter Three

Responsibility is a godly character quality that helps us discern what areas we are accountable for, and manage them with the understanding that the Lord is watching and will reward us for our efforts.

Marks of Responsibility

True responsibility is about responding to the ability God has placed in our hands. It's about responding to the grace He has given us. Actually, 'responsibility' can be rewritten as response-ability; doesn't that say it all?

In 1 Corinthians 15:10, Paul is very clear about acknowledging the grace empowering him—but he let that grace flow and extend into his actions. He responded to it. This is a great picture of response-ability.

> But by God's grace I am what I am, and His grace toward me was not ineffective. However, I worked more than any of them, yet not I, but God's grace that was with me. (HCSB)

In most cases, our ability to respond in appropriate ways is more important than what we are responding to! More than anything else, our responses to life's situations reveal our character, or the degree to which we are aligned with our true identity.

Self-Reliance vs. Responsibility

This distinction between self-reliance and responsibility falls on either side of a very thin line.

Biblical responsibility will always move us from self-reliance toward Christ-reliance! The bottom line difference, then, can usually be determined by honestly answering one question: who gets the credit when things go great? If our perceived successes act to bolster our self-esteem, and help us feel more worthy of the love and acceptance we seek, then we are relying on our performance and we are self-reliant. On the other hand, if we know the Lord is helping us in our successes and even in our failures, our reliance is on Christ.

The Apostle Paul wrote in 2 Corinthians 1:8-10,

> *For we do not want you to be unaware, brethren, of our affliction that came unto us in Asia; that we were burdened excessively, beyond our strength, so that we despaired even of life: indeed, we had the sentence of death within ourselves so that we would not trust in ourselves, but in God who raises the dead. (NAS)*

Paul's great troubles worked toward a great truth: his reliance was in Christ, not in himself! At first, this seems so straightforward and commonplace. However, the more gifted the individual, the more determined, the more equipped to serve God, the more the temptation to rely on self. Ironic, isn't it?

God gives us the gifts; then He encourages us to develop those gifts.

And yet, there is an accompanying tendency to rely on ourselves because we have the gifts and abilities to make things happen! The great truth that came to Paul—*"so that we would not trust in ourselves, but in God"* (2 Corinthians 1:9 NAS)— was information he had known for years. The knowledge had been transformed into revelation through the crucible of suffering.

When life seemed all but over for him, Paul came to a new experience of reliance on Christ's power.

The Default Setting: Self-Reliance

Self-reliance is the symptom of a greater, deeper problem: unbelief. "I don't believe that Jesus will take care of me, and I don't believe what He accomplished for me at the cross is enough..." This unbelief drives us to performance in order to provide for ourselves, our needs and our wants.

In some ways, self-reliance is a distortion, a problem of seeing clearly. We somehow misunderstand reality! In actual fact, without God intervening on my behalf every day, I am completely lost. Whether I understand it or not, I am constantly in desperate need for God. The surprising thing is that most days I'm not even aware of it.

Genuine reality, however, leads me towards a daily conscious awareness of my need for Jesus! The normal Christian progress of life, then, should develop humility and Christ-reliance, as I acknowledge God as the fountainhead and source of my life.

James Hudson Taylor, founder of the China Inland Mission, and a man mightily used by God, had a

revelation of truth from God's Word that came to
him after he served in China for a time. The
revelation was from John 15:5, *"Without Me, you
can do nothing"* (NKJV).

For the first time in his life, Hudson Taylor fully
understood and believed he was unable to
accomplish anything outside of Christ! His new
revelation led him to desperation for Christ!

Responsibility vs. Blame

A common natural inclination is to blame others for
our poor circumstances. What we fail to realize is
that this response of blaming robs us of our power
to live victorious lives! As soon as I blame other
people, or circumstances, or even fate for my
troubles, I turn myself into a victim who has no
control.

Nothing could be further from the truth!

Responsibility teaches me to take ownership of
every area of my life. As I do this, I no longer
blame others for the bad things in my life. Then,
circumstances out of my control become a new
opportunity to trust God as my Father (Matthew
6:9) and my Provider/Shepherd (Psalm 23).

The Bible tells us, *"the rain falls on the just and on
the unjust"* (Matthew 5:45).

Bad things happen to everyone. By acknowledging God, and thanking Him right in the middle of my circumstances—not just blaming Him *for* my circumstances—I begin to understand I have power through God in the midst of my troubles. Murmuring about poor circumstances, and complaining about bad luck only serve to make us feel powerless and victimized. On the contrary, responsibility turns the tables on victimization and makes me a major player in bringing success and joy into my life! I am responsible to thank God, and pray, and do what I can to have a great attitude throughout my circumstances.

Blaming people and problems is irresponsible. A clear understanding of boundaries (see Townsend and McLeod's book by the same title) helps us work through issues attached to responsibility! The boundaries idea is that I must clearly define what areas I am responsible for, and what I am not responsible for.

The Paralysis of Regret

Regret is another natural by-product of irresponsibility. When I am aware that I have not accomplished what I am responsible for, I lack fulfillment and joy, and begin to feel the weight of regret.

Imagine the Apostle Paul's feelings concerning his pre-Christian past when he persecuted and killed

Christians. Regret over his past actions could have paralyzed him. Rather than being mired in regret over his past sins, he dealt with them appropriately and then used thoughts from his past to motivate him toward greater surrender to Christ. *"Though I am least of all saints, … God's grace works more powerfully through me!"* (I Corinthians 15:9-10).

Responsibility and Change

Change and responsibility are closely related and often hang out with each other! They're like twins! Change empowers us to adapt to our circumstances—both outwardly and inwardly. Being able to respond (remember, response-ability), then, is being able to change!

The Boundary of Responsibility

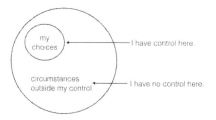

The inner circle (in the diagram) is labeled my choices, and it defines my responsibility. The outer circle is labeled circumstances outside of my control; things that happen here are not my responsibility.

In the outer circle I have no control; within the inner circle, I do have control. Imagine all of life in this way...

When we do, it starts to make sense that spending time talking, worrying, and being bothered about things in the outer circle is a waste of our time—because we can't affect any change: we have no control! What we can do, is make the right choices in our inner circle—our area of influence. The inner circle defines my boundary, my responsibility.

The inner circle defines my boundary of responsibility. With this in mind, shouldn't we try to have all of our conversations and attention brought within the inner circle?

When you think about it, there are people you know who seem to always want you to live and talk in the outer circle: they're always complaining about things over which they have no control. They fuss over other people's business and other people's choices; they complain about their government, their boss, their friends, their neighbours, and even their church, believe it or not! And watch out! They'll try to pull your conversations and interests and energies into the outer circle, too. Don't let them! Keep your focus and attention on things you can influence and change. Don't fall into the trap of worrying and complaining about things over which you have no influence. Pull everything back into the inner circle! If you can't bring it into the inner circle—you're wasting your time! In other words, if you can't change anything through words or actions, why complain about it?!

That being said, we still must remember that some things may be in the outer circle, where we have no control—but we still can pray and exert influence in the Spirit. In effect, we pull areas into our inner circle through prayer and intercession. We don't, however, complain, malign, or even talk negatively about things in the outer circle; we simply pray.

What Can You Do Right Now To Become More Responsible, and Less Self-Reliant?

✓ Begin an inventory of your conversations—ask someone to help you if this is difficult. Take notice of when you blame, murmur, or complain about anything! If you do, you are not being responsible! Blaming turns you into a helpless victim!

✓ Reflect back, and list people in your life who have helped you along the way (parents, teachers, mentors, friends). Self-reliance is taking credit for what you have done. Killing self-reliance happens as we acknowledge everything we have and everything we are is because of what God and others have put into our lives! So, take your list and write notes of gratitude to everyone.

✓ Draw inner and outer circles as we discussed them. Think about the three major areas of conflict and worry in your life. Identify which circle they belong in.

Notes and Next Steps

Forgiveness

Chapter Four

Forgiveness is one of the most powerful, most needed, yet most misunderstood concepts. To more fully understand its powerful applications, let's examine Jesus' words from the Lord's Prayer.

> *And forgive us our debts as we also have forgiven our debtors... For if you forgive people their wrongdoing, your heavenly Father will forgive you as well. But if you don't forgive people, your Father will not forgive your wrongdoing. (Matthew 6:12-15)*

At first glance, we might conclude this passage teaches forgiveness is a system of works and merit: if we forgive others, then we earn our own forgiveness. If we don't forgive, we can't earn forgiveness. This interpretation is a misunder-standing!

In this text, Jesus is making an observation, rather than defining a process for obtaining God's forgiveness. Jesus tells us that by harbouring unforgiveness, we erect a barrier around our hearts that prevents us from receiving the forgiveness God is so willing to extend to us!

Forgiving others sets us free from the bitterness and unforgiveness that is a barrier to the love and forgiveness of God.

In other words, when it comes to forgiveness if you can't give it, you can't get it!

It isn't difficult to see that forgiveness is a gift we give, not just to the one who has offended us, it is a gift we give ourselves!

"I Forgave Them, but I'm Still Angry!"

Perhaps you know people who have been offended or hurt by someone decades ago. Though they have said the words, "I forgive them", you know they haven't really forgiven. How can you tell? When they talk about the original incident (and, yes, they will talk about it!), you can clearly see and hear the same emotion and pain coming to the surface that they experienced when it all happened. The root of bitterness stayed lodged within the heart—and that's because there was no real forgiveness.

It's not that they didn't want to forgive: they may have said the words many times—but they did not fully grasp what forgiveness always demands.

Forgiveness Demands Placing My Hurts Inside the Boundary of God's Responsibility

First, let's talk about what forgiveness is not...

- **It's not a feeling or emotion.** Otherwise we'd have to wait until we felt something, or had an emotional experience to make us ready to extend forgiveness.

- **It's not just saying the words, "I forgive you".** Words are powerful as they are spoken with genuine faith. But without faith, words can also be spoken like some mystical incantation, thinking that the repetition of a magical phrase will bring the desired result. In the same way, voicing the words "I forgive you" won't work if we misunderstand what we're doing.

- **It's not only for the offender.** Forgiveness is as much about keeping my own heart clear and pure from bitterness as it is about extending forgiveness to someone who hurt me. Forgiveness is a complete letting go of expectation. It is establishing God's responsibility over the incident, and then guarding the boundaries of my heart so that I don't allow myself to take on again what I have determined is now God's responsibility.

In some sense, the dynamic of forgiveness is a subset of responsibility. Forgiving is really determining that I am no longer responsible for emotionally resolving a specific situation.

Let me say it as plainly as I can: when I forgive, I clearly and deliberately relinquish my rights for justice, for retribution, and for the emotional satisfaction of hearing the offender say to me, "I'm sorry—please forgive me, I was wrong!" Instead, I take my expectations and place them by faith under the responsibility of God. I give my rights and expectations to Him; how it all works out is now His responsibility. The result? Freedom!

People I know and love have been offended and hurt. Some of them have taken a position whereby they sincerely believe they have forgiven their offender, but are waiting for the day when their offender will return and say, "I'm sorry!" They are waiting to be proven right. This is not forgiveness.

Forgiveness Involves Taking Ownership of Offences

Consider Matthew 7:3-5.

> *Why do you look at the speck in your brother's eye but don't notice the log in your own eye? Or how can you say to your brother, 'Let me take the speck out of your eye,' and look, there's a log in your eye? Hypocrite! First take the log out of your eye, and then you will see clearly to take the speck out of your brother's eye. (HCSB)*

Jesus taught us to remove the log from our own eye before we attempt to remove the speck from our brother's eye. Jesus' words here can easily be applied to hurts, offences, and wrongdoing. By taking ownership of and responsibility for our part, we acknowledge that an offence might involve something we have done—and so we first need to look at ourselves, not at others.

When we take ownership for our actions, we don't even consider our brother's responsibility and his faults—only our own. So in a conflict where I am 20% at fault, I confess my full 20% fault (as clearly as I can) with no reference at all to my brother's 80% fault (that's the hard part!). I ask forgiveness by clearly acknowledging everything I have done wrong, regardless of *why* I did it! It's always tempting to explain why we did something wrong.

When we approach offences and hurts in this way, acknowledging our own wrong in order to clear our conscience, God's Spirit is well able to change the other person!

A Real Story of Forgiveness

I first learned this lesson a number of years ago after meeting a friend who left my church fifteen years earlier during a nasty church split. One-third of the church ended up leaving!

At the time of the split, this friend left; I stayed. Though I wasn't in any position of church leadership at the time, I wrote him a letter explaining why he was wrong to leave, and why I was right to stay! Well, that was fifteen years earlier. Then one day, here he was in front of me!

We talked politely for a few minutes, and then parted company. Within a short time of our parting, the Holy Spirit strongly impressed upon me that I needed to contact him and ask his forgiveness! Imagine my surprise! Yet I knew the Holy Spirit was speaking, and a Scripture popped into my mind: *"By this shall all men know you are my disciples, that you have love one for another"* (John 13:35).

Note what it does not say: they'll know you're my disciples because you're always right. As I thought of the church-split, I was defending a position—I wasn't concerned about love at all!

It was only just then, after fifteen years, that I realized how badly I had handled the situation with this letter I had written. Never once had I asked my friend why he left the church, what issues troubled him, or how his concerns had been addressed. Instead, my letter of fifteen years earlier was basically a declaration that he was wrong and I was right.

I called him up, and within a few days we met again. I imagine he was quite surprised when I asked his forgiveness for my prideful attitude. I acknowledged how unlike Christ I had been. You see, fifteen years earlier I wasn't concerned about him—I was only concerned about establishing that I was right in staying at the church. I was not concerned about being like Jesus, about forgiving, or about the spiritual well-being of people who left during the church split. Jesus would have thought about all these things!

I'm happy to say my friend was very gracious to forgive me and my offensive attitudes of the past. What happened next was a complete surprise!

This same friend approached the pastor of the church (the one he had left during the split) and asked for forgiveness for offenses *he had himself committed* while leaving fifteen years earlier! Wow!

Then, the following day, he came to me again, and said these words: "Jim, after you asked me to forgive you—for the first time in fifteen years I realized I had also done something wrong!" This began a journey of forgiveness that has proven to be powerful and therapeutic for many people. "Please forgive me" can be a tremendously liberating phrase!

As a father, I have personally felt the alienation separating a rather rebellious teenaged son from a rather angry father (that would be me)! An argument stemming from a son's bad attitude, intersecting with my own anger created a broken relationship! Here's the difficulty: it was his fault—that is, until I got angry—then it became my fault. When my temper cooled, the Lord reminded me about the story of the speck and the log.

How could I correct my son without correcting myself, first? So I went to my son, and said: "Would you forgive me? I overreacted. I never should have gotten angry like that—I'm really sorry." Then I gave him a hug, and received his gracious forgiveness (my kids are great at forgiving!) In that act of forgiveness came a new love and appreciation for each other that wasn't there before!

What Can You Do Right Now To Build Forgiveness Into Your Life?

✓ Catalogue your past hurts. When you describe what happened to you, does the emotion and hurt resurface and open the wound again? If so, you probably have not forgiven!

✓ Are there people that make you angry as you think about them? It may be that you need to forgive.

✓ Is there someone you can't look in the eye, because you know they have something against you? Is it time to have that difficult conversation, and determine if you need to take ownership over something?

✓ Perhaps the person you need to forgive is not available to you. (You don't know where they are or they may have died.) If this is so, write a letter of forgiveness on the following Notes and Next Steps page.

Notes and Next Steps

_____

_____

_____

_____

_____

_____

_____

_____

_____

_____

_____

_____

_____

_____

_____

_____

Spiritual Warfare

Chapter Five

From Jim's journal:

October 17, 2013 ... I find myself waiting for the Holy Spirit to do something ... I'm starting to realize He's waiting for me! I must make sure I don't try to make things easy for myself or others: my job isn't to make things easy, it is to make things CLEAR! Reflecting on Ephesians 6 (our spiritual battle and spiritual armour): Some say, "I'm going to put 'them' in their place! ... I'll show them a thing or two! I'm going to win this argument!" Yeah, you may win ... but the Kingdom loses!

There are many wonderful books that tackle the topic of spiritual warfare; this chapter treats the discussion differently. I am simply focusing on an often-overlooked strategy of spiritual warfare that is both practical and powerful: prayer. I'll present a prayer strategy that blends three Scriptures on warfare.

The MMA of the Spirit!

The spiritual warfare we are involved in requires mastery of many forms of "fighting". Some fighters are boxers; some are wrestlers; some focus on grappling with arm, leg, and hand submission holds; still others practice judo or karate, or other variations of the martial arts. In the last decade, the fighting world has seen the rise of MMA—Mixed Martial Arts—all forms of fighting combined!

Today Christians need the spiritual equivalent of the Mixed Martial Arts to become formidable Christian warriors! What I am offering you from God's Word is a mixture of three strategies which combine to make a very effective weapon that will equip you to win your battles.

1. **Jesus' Example**
Jesus fought the devil after 40 days of fasting by quoting Scriptures.
2. **Our Spiritual Weapons**
The Ephesian church was taught to fight using spiritual weapons and armour. Specifically, to

engage faith as a shield to stop fiery arrows from the devil. The sword of the Spirit is the only offensive weapon listed!

3. **Thoughts**

The Corinthian church was taught to fight by bringing every thought into obedience to Christ.

Let's use all three strategies to focus our attention on the main arena of conflict: our mind. Scripture teaches us that our carnal, natural mind is against God; the process of allowing the Holy Spirit to change our thinking by bringing truth from God's Word into our mind is referred to as *"renewing our mind"* (Romans 12:2). For God's Word to have its full impact, all lies, faulty imaginations, and incorrect ways of thinking must be removed from our mind.

> *Since the weapons of our warfare are not worldly, but are powerful through God for the demolition of strongholds. We demolish arguments and every high-minded thing that is raised up against the knowledge of God, taking every thought captive to obey Christ."* (2 Corinthians 10:4-6 HCSB)

The Battle Field of the Mind

Most Christians have never learned to control their thoughts. As a result, wrong thinking is established that becomes a mental stronghold. A stronghold is a lie that takes root and—if not challenged—will eventually affect every other area of thinking. A stronghold is devastating.

Consider the woman who has a stronghold in her thinking that was first established as a result of sexual abuse as a child. The stronghold may be a lie that says all men are abusive, perverted, and sex is evil. Unless the lie is uprooted and God's truth is introduced, this thinking will ruin her life and derail God's potential for her.

A number of years ago, I was sharing the Gospel with a woman with a different mental stronghold. She said to me, "Jim, I can believe that Jesus loves everyone else in the world—but I can't believe He loves me." This woman was hindered by a lie; a stronghold in her thinking. What a devastating thing to believe about yourself!

Let's turn our attention to our three strategies of warfare. We find them in well-known Scriptures that provide the truth we need to be equipped to fight these lies and strongholds.

1. Jesus' Example of Warfare

Matthew 4:3-11

> During that time the devil came and said to him, "If you are the Son of God, tell these stones to become loaves of bread." But Jesus told him, "No! The Scriptures say, 'People do not live by bread alone, but by

every word that comes from the mouth of God.' Then the devil took him to the holy city, Jerusalem, to the highest point of the Temple, and said, "If you are the Son of God, jump off! For the Scriptures say, 'He will order his angels to protect you. And they will hold you up with their hands so you won't even hurt your foot on a stone." *Jesus responded, "The Scriptures also say, 'You must not test the LORD your God.'" Next the devil took him to the peak of a very high mountain and showed him all the kingdoms of the world and their glory. "I will give it all to you," he said, "if you will kneel down and worship me."*

"Get out of here, Satan," Jesus told him. "For the Scriptures say, 'You must worship the LORD your God and serve only him.'" Then the devil went away, and angels came and took care of Jesus.

Jesus responded to the devil's temptations—the spiritual attacks—by quoting Scriptures that relate to the area of temptation! If Jesus did it—we can do it too!

"If you are a Christian, you are at war. But our approach to spiritual warfare usually falls into one of two extremes - either we place an undue emphasis on Satan and his powers or we completely ignore the existence of a personal enemy."

-Chip Ingram [11]

---

11   Chip Ingram, *The Invisible War*. Ada, Michigan: Baker Publishing Group, 2008.

2. Our Weapons

Ephesians 6:10-18

> *A final word: Be strong in the Lord and in his mighty power. Put on all of God's armour so that you will be able to stand firm against all strategies of the devil. For we are not fighting against flesh-and-blood enemies, but against evil rulers and authorities of the unseen world, against mighty powers in this dark world, and against evil spirits in the heavenly places.*
>
> *Therefore, put on every piece of God's armour so you will be able to resist the enemy in the time of evil. Then after the battle you will still be standing firm. Stand your ground, putting on the belt of truth and the body armour of God's righteousness. For shoes, put on the peace that comes from the Good News so that you will be fully prepared. In addition to all of these, hold up the shield of faith to stop the fiery arrows of the devil. Put on salvation as your helmet, and take the sword of the Spirit, which is the word of God.*
>
> *Pray in the Spirit at all times and on every occasion. Stay alert and be persistent in your prayers for all believers everywhere.*

Interestingly, Paul mentioned three pieces of armour, and then emphasizes the next piece—the shield: "In addition to these, hold up the shield of faith to stop all the fiery arrows." The shield of faith is the one piece of armour most emphasized in the MMA of the Spirit!

3. Thoughts—The Principal Arena of Conflict

2 Corinthians 10:4-5

> For the weapons of our warfare are not carnal but mighty in God for pulling down strongholds, casting down arguments and every high thing that exalts itself against the knowledge of God, bringing every thought into captivity to the obedience of Christ.

Here the Corinthian church is called to captivate thoughts that have become strongholds!

Together, all these verses teach us:

- We must access our faith (the shield from Ephesians 6) to stop the fiery arrows (lies of the evil one) from hitting us. If we are hit, the devil's lies affect us—we become discouraged, then disillusioned, then depressed and, if we eventually give up the fight, we could even succumb to despair.

- The weapons at our disposal are powerful! When used properly, they allow us to bring every thought into "the obedience of Christ". In other words, we can take negative thoughts, tempting thoughts, and bring them under control.

- Our mind is the arena of conflict. The evil one always attacks with lies—half-truths, innuendos, and slanderous comments about God's ways. We respond with truth!

A Strategy for Victory in Warfare

Using the truth of the Scriptures listed above, and following Jesus' example, leads us to the following strategy. When we are attacked by a thought (a lie, or untruth):

1. **Quote a Specific Scripture** Choose a Scripture that is related to the attack (like Jesus did!)

2. **Personalize the Scripture** Put it in the first person to make it your own. You engage your faith when you believe the truth of this Scripture is for you! You are lifting up a shield to stop and put out the fiery arrow from Satan.

3. **Pray for an Unsaved Loved One** You are now advancing on the devil's kingdom—attacking using the sword. When you pray,

ask that the truth of God's Word also becomes true for your unsaved loved one.

For many years, I was plagued with the thought that, sometime in the future, I would deny the Lord and fall into sin. I would fight the thought and try not to entertain it but it seemed to linger on the edge of my thinking and occasionally popped up to bother me. Then I applied this strategy and found total deliverance from the thought!

Here's how I applied it:

1. When the thought came I quoted Jude 1:24 aloud: *"Now unto Him that is able to keep you from falling, and present you faultless before the presence of His glory"* (NKJV).

2. I personalized it: "Lord, you are the One who is able to prevent me from falling into sin, and to make me faultless! Thank You!"

3. Then I prayed for my friend, Joe: "And now, Lord, I pray for Joe, my unsaved friend. I'm asking You to work in his life so that he also can become faultless before You! Jesus, save him from his sins and help him see Your great love for him. Amen!"

This three-step process has helped many, many people get free from strongholds that kept them captivated. Use it and become free from thoughts that bring fear and bondage! It really works!

Another Real Life Story of Spiritual Warfare

The following question was sent in to our website (www.the-intimate-couple.com). Notice how our reply uses the same steps to deal with wrong, unbiblical thoughts and to remove strongholds.

Question:

I was a virgin when my wife and I married last year. My wife was not. She had several lovers before coming to Christ, and one after. She was honest and shared that with me. She's tried repeatedly to tell me she's broken all soul ties with them. So why can't I 'get over it'?

I can't even put into words what I feel: anger, sadness, betrayal, which all seems strange, right, since it was before me? Please tell me what I can do to deal with this.

Note that this husband has a plaguing thought that is derived from a lie, or stronghold, in his thinking. From what we are told, it seems the *wife's* sin has been dealt with, and that the husband has a forgiveness problem.

Answer:

In answering your question, we are assuming that your wife's sexual history is not hindering her, and that her past sexual relationships have been dealt with and she is experiencing freedom. If it is still an issue with her, we suggest she reads The Invisible Bond, by Barbara Wilson.

There are two things we think you need:

You need a change of perspective. *All of us are broken to some degree. Some, like your wife, have obvious outward areas of brokenness. Others of us have them in our hearts. When we understand this concept it's easier to forgive, and be forgiving.*

You may have been a virgin, but that doesn't mean that your life has been free from sexual sin.
Think about it: what man has not lusted when looking at women—actual or virtual! You are in your mid-30's. Do you realize how many thousands of images of girls may have played through your mind—even if it was only for a fleeting moment?

Jesus said that lusting after a woman is equivalent to adultery in our hearts. Is it reasonable to imagine that all of the women you have "lusted after", even momentarily, might weigh heavily on your wife's mind?

As well, rather than focusing on what you're struggling with, consider what your wife may be struggling with! Is she wondering how much you love and accept her because of her past sexual relationships and your inability to forget? Your wife may not feel sexually confident with you because of her past.

You need to adopt a strategy to deal with your thoughts. *Fighting them is like playing "tug-of-war" with the devil; you can never win. You must drop the rope! You do that by using the troubling thought (of your wife's previous sexual partners) as a springboard to new thoughts based on Scriptural truth!*

When we are dealing with thoughts that seem to torment us, we have to see they are thoughts originating from the devil—the enemy of our soul. He wants to rob, steal, and destroy your marriage (John 10:10) as well as the great things God has done by bringing you together with your wife. These thoughts are the flaming darts the Bible warns against in Ephesians 6:16.

Our response is to lift up the shield of faith! This means you must engage your faith by proclaiming what God says—regardless of how you feel. In 1 John 1:9 we're told when someone confesses their sin, He forgives and washes them clean and so that is what happened to your wife! She is clean from the past and you have to learn to adopt a strategy that helps you exercise your faith and confess the truth—what God says. **This process**

will result in you being free from all of the thoughts that torment you.

When a thought about your wife's past sexual relationships comes to you, there are 3 steps to follow:

Step 1: Quote a Scripture related to the thought of your wife's past sin and sexual partners, aloud.

Step 2: Personalize the verse, and say it aloud in the "first person".

Step 3: Then pray for an unsaved loved one, aloud.

OK, let's put the steps into practice now. The thought comes to you...

Step 1: Quote 1 John 1:9 "If we confess our sin, He is faithful and righteous to forgive us, and cleanse us from all unrighteousness."

Step 2: Personalize the verse, by putting it in your own words. "Lord, thank you that Mary (put in your wife's name) confessed her sin—and I have confessed my sin—and that you have totally forgiven us and cleansed us from all wrong! Thank You, Jesus!"

Step 3: Pray for an unsaved loved one (always pray for the same person). "And now I pray for our neighbours, Bob and Alice (put in names of unsaved friends or loved ones), and I pray that they may experience the same forgiveness we have experienced. Amen!"

Many experts agree it takes three weeks to form a habit. Be diligent to take these three steps and get into the habit of thinking this new way. We guarantee you will be free and your marriage will take on a new joy!

What Can You Do Right Now To Engage In Spiritual Warfare?

✓ Commit 2 Corinthians 10:4-6 to memory.

✓ Identify areas of habitual sin. First, confess it to an accountability partner. If you don't have someone like this—find someone! Second, find an appropriate Scripture to recite every time this temptation comes to you. Then work through the three steps listed above!

Notes and Next Steps

_____

_____

_____

_____

_____

_____

_____

_____

_____

_____

_____

_____

_____

_____

_____

Facing Your Fears

Chapter Six

All of us have fears to deal with at some time or another.

For some, paralysis caused by fears becomes a normal way of life: a rather wretched way of life, but a way of life nevertheless. Many of us suffer from fear of failure and fear of disclosure, to name just a few.

Although fear may not be rational, it is very real!

Real Stories of Fear

A young friend of ours, a teenager at the time, died tragically in a drowning accident. Shortly after that event, Carrie stepped into the shower and as the water hit her face she imagined what it must have been like for our friend in the last moments of his life as he was drowning. Her imagination caused the adrenalin to take over and Carrie could feel her heart beating faster as she sensed a wave of fear washing over her. All it took was a step to the left or right moving her face out of the stream of water and the fear ended.

It all happened in just a moment, so end of story, right? Wrong!

Carrie's fear could be stopped in a second, so it wasn't important, right? Wrong again!

Actually, this identical scenario of imagination, thoughts, and then real fear repeated itself again and again every morning for years!

One day I received a call from an old acquaintance who was rather distraught. This young man was plagued by a thought—a fear—that he had committed the unpardonable sin. My friend could not be convinced otherwise because this thought was so entrenched in his thinking. He was on the verge of a nervous breakdown. He couldn't work. He was visiting doctors, psychiatrists, and ministers—and still he was not free from his fear!

What happened to resolve these cases of debilitating fear? Applying the same simple three step process we discussed in the last chapter (the Mixed Martial Arts of the Spirit) brought total freedom from fear!

1. Quote a Scripture related to the fear.

2. Personalize the Scripture, put it in your own words, and say it aloud for yourself to hear.

3. Pray for an unsaved loved one!

When Carrie became aware that the devil was trying mess her up she started to apply the spiritual MMA process where it is important to end by praying for someone else. Carrie chose to pray for the parents who lost their son to drowning. Within less than two weeks, Carrie was free. Those thoughts and imaginations of drowning were totally gone and have never returned.

As for my friend, he faithfully applied these steps and within a few weeks, his clarity of thought returned. Eventually he was totally delivered from his plaguing thoughts. He regained his health, attended and graduated from a Bible College, married a beautiful Christian girl, "and lived happily ever after"!

For some people, the fears are right up on the surface. For others, the fears are often unspoken and lurk far below the surface. In these cases, we have to face our fears and put them on the table!

"If the Lord be with us, we have no cause of fear. His eye is upon us, His arm over us, His ear open to our prayer - His grace sufficient, His promise unchangeable."

– John Newton [12]

---

12   John Newton, *The Works of John Newton: Volume 1.* Philedelphia, 1839.

Slam Those Fears on the Table!

As I described in Chapter Six, I have had a secret fear that I would someday sin and fall away from the Lord. It always seemed to be lurking in the shadows and nagging at me. Then one day, I decided I needed to take my hidden fears—and face them!

I actually got a piece of paper and wrote down the top three things I was afraid of, one of them being this fear of falling away. As soon as I wrote that fear down, a Scripture came to my mind:

> Now unto Him that is able to keep you from falling, and present you faultless before the presence of His glory with exceeding joy. (Jude 1:24 NKJV)

All of a sudden I realized that I didn't have to fear I would ever fall—because God was able to keep me from falling! By facing our fears with God's Word of truth, we will be delivered from our fears! At this point, as I mentioned before, whenever the thought returned—I used the three step MMA process to totally defeat it.

What Can You Do Right Now To Face Your Fears?

✓ Pray for the Lord's guidance, and reflect about your life, asking this question: What things do I really fear? Your answers may seem silly at first—but fear is not rational!

✓ Write the fears on a piece of paper in front of you, and then pray again. "Lord, Your Word says, *'There is no fear in love; instead, perfect love drives out fear, because fear involves punishment'*" (I John 4:18 HCSB). Look for Scriptures that deal specifically with your fears and pray them aloud!

✓ Learn the three step MMA process and teach someone else who struggles with thoughts.
  1. Quote Scripture
  2. Personalize it
  3. Pray for an unsaved loved one

Notes and Next Steps

_____

_____

_____

_____

_____

_____

_____

_____

_____

_____

_____

_____

_____

_____

_____

_____

_____

The Power of the
Secret Life

Chapter Seven

I love the words of the song that says,

No guilt in life, no fear in death,

This is the power of Christ in me![13]

The beauty of these words is found in the depth of their truth.

---

13   Keith Getty and Stewart Townend. In Christ Alone. Getty Music, 2001.

The Secret Life: Victory Over Sin

Do you have secret sin?

There is one way to experience victory; confess your secret sin to someone you trust!

> *Therefore confess your sins to one another and pray for one another, so that you may be healed. (James 5:16)*

I remember the days when I would avoid this verse, because I didn't like it! I knew God forgave me when I confessed my sin to Him—but real victory over hidden sin never happened until I confessed my sin to someone else. That is when healing started to take place!

In my personal life, I began the discipline of confession a number of years ago. Having an accountability partner, who has the freedom to ask the *hard questions,* is life-changing and liberating! Though establishing and continuing this kind of relationship will most likely be the hardest thing you'll ever do—it will also be one of the best things you'll ever do!

The Secret Life: Producing Power

OK, so how do we produce power from our secret life?

Power to live an abundant, Christian life is generated from the power of a clear conscience! A clear conscience is the result of mastery over our secret life, our hidden life. With no secret sins putting the brakes on your Christian life, you will lunge forward in God!

Listen to this:

> *Now the goal of our instruction is love that comes from a pure heart, a good conscience, and a sincere faith.*
> *(I Timothy 1:5 HCSB)*

Cleaning up the secret area of your life will be the biggest battle you've ever fought—but it will change *your heart*, improve *your conscience* (your mind), and require you to exercise *your faith* (your spirit)! But wait! These three elements of heart, conscience, and faith are the end goals of our walk with Christ!

Attaining all three of the goals listed here is like a high-performance custom car firing on all cylinders! When your heart, mind, and spirit are firing on all cylinders, you've got some serious power, and you're going places!

What Can You Do Right Now To Gain Power in Your Secret Life?

✓ Get an accountability partner and bare your soul! There is no easy way to do this! If it's easy for you, that means you didn't do it right!

✓ Confess everything. You must work hard to get a clean conscience—don't leave anything unconfessed. One little thing that you don't deal with will come back to haunt you!

✓ Establish regular times of accountability. Every other week, I meet with my personal pastor, to be accountable. Set up meeting times every week, or every other week. Don't let the times between your meetings be any longer.

Notes and Next Steps

_____

_____

_____

_____

_____

_____

_____

_____

_____

_____

_____

_____

_____

_____

_____

Finances

Chapter Eight

From Jim's journal:

October 17, 2013

... It seems that God operates on the frequency of relationships. When Father provides, get ready - He is generous! If you - imperfect parents - know how to give good gifts, how much more your heavenly Father? (Matthew 7:11)

June 5, 2013

... Got a call from a lady from another church: she decided she's going to start tithing to our church

because *"she likes the way we spend our money"!
Wow!*

When I started really honestly examining my life, there was one area that clearly revealed the need for no-default living, it was in the area of our finances.

As I mentioned earlier, for many years I simply assumed the Lord would take care of my family's finances, and it didn't really matter what I was being paid, God would provide. After all, I was faithful to tithe 10% of my income as well as give offerings over and above that amount. The assumption that the Lord would provide was (and still is) true. What was missing from my life, though, was an accompanying decision to rigorously get ahold of our finances and develop a financial plan for our future. I could have—but I didn't; instead, I chose to live by default—assuming it would all work out in the end. It didn't.

Understand, we have nine children and have been in Christian ministry—first Christian school education, and then pastoring—for thirty two years. Not too many years ago, we found ourselves thousands of dollars in consumer debt, and with no appreciable assets! I felt like part of my life came screeching to a halt as the terrible consequences of living by default in the area of finances came painfully into view!

Funny isn't it? I say, we "found ourselves thousands of dollars in consumer debt". It sounds as if everything was going along just fine until we stumbled into some trap that immediately and radically changed things for us! That's not how it happened. Actually, we ended up in debt because I was living by default. I had no plan, no practical budget, no emergency fund, and no one to show us how we should do it differently. I certainly didn't have a strategy to get us out! It was my fault, plain and simple. I was living by default, hoping that it would all work out.

Reflecting back, there have been stages of learning that took place, and I'd like to mention the resources that have been the most influential:

1. The Blessed Life DVD series, by Robert Morris

2. Walking in Financial Freedom DVD series, by Earl Pitts

3. Financial Peace University (FPU) DVD series, by Dave Ramsey

FPU has been the most effective tool for us; the rigorous application of the biblical principles behind Dave Ramsey's FPU has really made the difference for us most recently. Praise God, today we are out of debt, have accumulated some savings, and have an emergency fund!

More than any other area, it is in my finances where I struggle with feelings of regret: I have friends my age who already have their houses paid off!

Living by default has also brought some financial hardship to my children—for example, I have no education saving funds for their education, and have limited the options available to them.

Now, one beautiful thing about walking with Jesus is that He is able to turn the bad things around, and actually use them for good—and that is my prayer! Nevertheless, living by default is costly!

Let's say you are in a situation now similar to where I was a few years ago; your finances are a mess, you have debt (outside your house mortgage), you don't want to talk about your problem, and even try to justify it somehow. In a phrase, you are living by default!

"If a person gets his attitude toward money straight, it will help straighten out almost every other area in his life."

– Billy Graham [14]

---

14 http://billygraham.org/grow-your-faith/topics/health-lifestyle/money/

What Can You Do Right Now to Start Living a No-Default Financial Life?

- ✓ If you're not tithing, start today; otherwise you're robbing God of what belongs to Him (not a good thing to do!)

- ✓ Enroll in Dave Ramsey's Financial Peace University: check his website (www.daveramsey.com) to find a course offered near you. Read his books, listen to his podcasts and start to think differently. Aggressively begin the "7 Baby Steps" today!

- ✓ Read and pray through the Book of Proverbs in the Bible. You'll get a solid sensing of how God has designed compassionate capitalism; you'll learn volumes about wealth, riches, and money.

Notes and Next Steps

_____

_____

_____

_____

_____

_____

_____

_____

_____

_____

_____

_____

_____

_____

_____

Marriage

Chapter Nine

If you had to choose just one area in your life where you could practice no-default living, it should be in your marriage! Fortunately, we don't have to make those kinds of choices. We can experience no-default living in all areas of our lives!

Of all human relationships, marriage is the most important. In fact, marriage is the most important institution, relationship, enterprise, and covenant on earth! It is a masterpiece of Divine creativity, and the very citadel of intellectual, emotional, spiritual, and sexual intimacy. Within the framework of this holy union, Heaven comes to earth!

From this perspective, it is no wonder that the devil, the enemy of our souls, is working overtime to destroy God's most wonderful arrangement! Some of the enemy's most effective weapons are our ignorance, our selfishness, and our misinformation garnered from this fallen world.

Ignorance, selfishness, and misinformation will result from living your marriage by default. Most newlyweds naively think everything will work out "because we love each other so much". Remember, no-default living is a life by design. A marriage lived by design is a marriage based on the Scriptural pattern given us in the Bible! Contrary to what some misinformed people believe, the Bible is one hot marriage manual!

Following God's design, husbands cherish wives with self-sacrificing love and wives, in turn, genuinely honour their husbands; both husbands and wives enjoy each other and develop authentic intimacy spiritually, intellectually, emotionally, and sexually. Of course, this kind of marriage does take hard work and planning—but it is so worth it!

"I have known many happy marriages, but never a compatible one. The whole aim of marriage is to fight through and survive the instant when incompatibility becomes unquestionable."

– G.K. Chesterton [15]

---

15   G.K. Chesterton, *What's Wrong with the World*. Fairfield, Iowa: 1st World Library, 2006.

Carrie and I have been married for thirty-two years now (we're also parents to nine kids and grandparents to eight wonderful kids, with one more on the way!) and we have always had an exceptionally good marriage. We've avoided some heartache that other couples work through by following the Lord's ways as much as we knew how. Yet, in the last eight years of our marriage, there have been some dramatic improvements in what we would have described as an already great marriage!

The Intimacy Iceberg

Why the improvement? In the last few years, Carrie and I have been intentionally developing intimacy! Most people think *sex* when they hear the word "intimacy". In actual fact, intimacy is like an iceberg; what people see of the iceberg is just a small part of what is actually there.

We have all heard that the tip of an iceberg (what can be seen above the surface of the water) is only about 10% of the entire structure. What lies beneath the surface of the water is massive compared to what is visible to the eye. In the same way, sex is only the top 10% of intimacy; what is *under* the surface in your relationship makes all the difference.

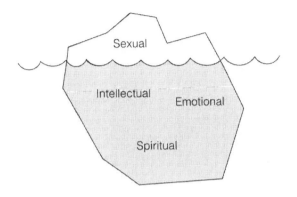

No-Default Intimacy Explained

Below the surface of all fulfilling, sexual relationships are authentic emotional, intellectual, and spiritual connections. Remember, sex is just the tip of the intimacy iceberg!

A truly intimate relationship is made up of four types of intimacy:

1. **Emotional Intimacy.** It is in this particular area of closeness that romance best fits into the picture. When our emotions are involved, things get very interesting! It's all the warm, cozy feelings of falling in love and being in love that we think of when we consider emotional intimacy. All of the words, thoughts, and actions that affect

how we feel about our spouse and about our marriage have a bearing on emotional intimacy. The best word to use? Romance!

2. **Intellectual Intimacy.** Intellectual intimacy may well be the most overlooked form of intimacy. Nevertheless, it is this intellectual closeness that often first connects two people together. Granted, a man may be attracted by the physical appearance of a woman and vice versa, but it is the closeness developed through getting to know each other intellectually that first draws a couple to each other. Many couples feel that "spark" of excitement growing between them as they spend time conversing and getting to know each other. This process begins intellectually and quickly becomes emotional as well.

    Over time, April and Doug fell madly in love with each other; however, if you were to look at them they seem oddly matched with each other. Doug is a big outgoing guy from rural Canada, and April is a shy, very petite girl from Southeastern Asia. How did they ever hook up? The internet. Doug and April met online and began a courtship in cyberspace!

    How can something like this work? It can work, because "falling in love" is most often started by developing intellectual intimacy through conversation!

3. **Spiritual Intimacy.** Based on the bedrock of common values and beliefs, spiritual intimacy extends our oneness to the very core of who we are, and influences how we perceive ourselves and the world around us. Arguably the most neglected form of intimacy, spiritual intimacy is also the most important, because it is a tri-intimacy involving husband, wife, and God. Our relationship with God is like the hub of a wheel. Everything else in life comes into balance when the Lord has a central position in our life. In our marriage vows, husband and wife make a vow to each other and also to God. Our vows include Him. With this understanding, as we grow closer to our spouse spiritually, we also grow closer to God. Don't have a marriage lived by default! Do everything you can to experience a no-default marriage!

4. **Sexual Intimacy.** The other forms of intimacy can be experienced between any two people; however, it is sexual intercourse, reserved between husband and wife, that makes marriage the most unique of all relationships. In sex, man and wife are made one flesh.

Why is there a much higher rate (more than 50% higher) of separation between lovers when they cohabitate, as opposed to their married counterparts? One factor is that the commitment of marriage provides the best context for intimacy: sexual and otherwise.

What Can You Do to Start Having a No-Default Marriage Right Now?

✓ Together with your spouse, begin reading the articles from our website www.the-intimate-couple.com, a site dedicated to the development of intimacy in marriages. It's important that you both spend time reading and discussing. Wonderful things will happen when you are engaged in no-default marriage development!

✓ Check out our e-book, *The 7-Day Sex Challenge.* It is a week-long course structured around Scriptural teaching concerning commitment, vows, God's design for marriage, forgiveness, rewinding, and sex! If you follow through for seven days, it will change your life and marriage!

Notes and Next Steps

_____

_____

_____

_____

_____

_____

_____

_____

_____

_____

_____

_____

_____

_____

_____

Prayer

Chapter Ten

Prayer is one of the most basic parts of living a Christian life. My goal, then, is to encourage you to experience prayer by intention and not by default.

Default Prayer

For most of us, praying by default means there is no intention, no purpose, no plan guiding us; instead, we live in constant reaction mode. We let other people or, more likely outside circumstances drive us. Prayer? Well, we pray when we have to pray: before meals, during emergencies, and whenever we remember to shoot up a quick request.

Does that pretty well sum up your normal experience of prayer? If so, you are living one of the most critical parts of your life by default, and it's time to recalibrate what normal means!

No-Default Prayer

Intentional, purposeful prayer is not rushed or squeezed into an already hectic schedule, leaving the leftovers from a busy day for God. It is planned, regular, and significant. My journey towards no-default prayer began in earnest years ago while on a retreat in Mexico with my wife. We stayed with a wonderful lady who was well known in her region for being a prayer warrior and intercessor. Together with a group of close friends, she would spend hours seeking God, and hearing His voice. Praying with her and her team for that week gave me a desire to sustain the prayer life I experienced then.

To do so has required three things from me:

1. Placing a higher personal value on prayer in my life

2. Getting up earlier

3. Finding prayer partners to pray with

Your list of required things may be different from mine—but whatever is necessary for you, do it!

No-Default Metaphors for Prayer

Over the past few decades, there have been a number of prayer metaphors that have proved helpful and encouraging to me as I've considered effective prayer:

1. The Prayer Funnel

I first remember hearing about the prayer funnel as a young Christian, during a sermon. I don't remember where I was, or who was speaking, but the illustration endures.

As we pray for the salvation of individuals, we may not see anything change in their lives outwardly. In the spirit-realm, however, there are amazing things beginning to happen: God has placed them into His funnel!

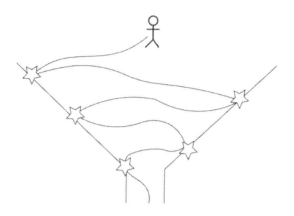

The outer edges of the funnel represent the situations, circumstances, events, and people that God providentially puts in front of them as we pray—and they bump into these situations and people and career off and react—often going in the opposite direction! It might be a Christian witnessing to them, a car accident making them see their mortality, or perhaps a Scripture verse comes to their mind.

Whatever the circumstance, God gets their attention, and softens their hearts. In a natural funnel, whatever is bouncing back and forth on the walls of the funnel also moves downward to the apex—the spout of the funnel—because of gravity. In this image of the prayer funnel as we pray for the person, the will of God is relentlessly pulling her downward toward the apex. At the apex, she becomes saved!

For some it may take a lot of time, but no-default prayer is continuous and purposeful and does not give up. Eventually, when the individual has reached the apex of the funnel, the prevailing drawing and wooing of the Spirit of God is easier to give in to than to cling to their own rebellion!

2. The Siege of Love

In siege warfare, a city is surrounded by opposing forces who camp, not allowing anyone in or out. It is simply a matter of time before the siege is over. Siege warfare is not the most exciting mode of fighting between opposing forces, it is, however, the most effective!

In the Old Testament when Joshua was leading the nation of Israel into the Promised Land, they had to fight and displace a number of resident nations. God revealed to Joshua the strategy to use when his troops came face-to-face with a fortified city. This strategy is given to us in Deuteronomy: *"If [a city] does not make peace with you but wages war against you, lay siege to it"* (20:12 HCSB). What worked for Joshua so many years ago physically, is meant to provide a lesson for us today spiritually!

Romans 5:14 says:

> For whatever was written in the past was written for our instruction, so that we may have hope through endurance and through the encouragement from the Scriptures. (HCSB)

Joshua's battles were natural; ours are spiritual (although, often with very natural implications!).

Ephesians 6 indicates to us:

> Our battle is not against flesh and blood, but against the rulers, against the authorities, against the world powers of this darkness, against the spiritual forces of evil in the heavens. (6:12 HCSB)

So, we aren't fighting people, we are fighting spiritual forces that hold people captive!

In Deuteronomy 20, it was never a question of if the city would capitulate; it was a matter of when the city would capitulate! The final outcome was never in question.

Spiritually speaking, siege warfare involves praying that Jesus' arms will surround the person you're praying for, so that everywhere they go they'll bump into Jesus! Praying a siege around someone spiritually is to surround them with prayer so they can no longer run away from God!

When we present the Gospel to people, it is as if we are approaching a fortified city. Many times, people won't respond to the Gospel right away—they may even resist. As it was with Joshua, the Lord wants us to begin praying for them and lay a siege around these people in the spiritual sense, perhaps something like the following prayer:

> *Lord, I pray for Joe right now. I'm asking you to lay a siege of love around Joe. Put your arms around him, so that everywhere he goes, he will bump into you, Lord! Surround him! In the circumstances and situations of life reveal the truth of who you are to him. Surround Him, Jesus I pray! Amen.*

"When we depend upon organizations, we get what organizations can do; when we depend upon education, we get what education can do; when we depend upon man, we get what man can do; but when we depend upon prayer, we get what God can do."

–A.C. Dixon [16]

---

16 Piper, John. *Brothers We Are Not Professionals.* Qtd. B&H Publishing Group, 2002.

What Can You Do Right Now To Begin No-Default Prayer?

✓ Set aside thirty minutes a day, five days a week to pray. This probably won't happen unless you are meeting someone else to pray with you. Do whatever you have to do to make it work! If you don't have this kind of no-default prayer life now, what makes you think you'll be able to change? You need help, or you would have done it yourself already!

✓ Make up a prayer list of people you need to pray for every day. Change the way you pray, and what you pray for them each day so that your prayers don't become repetitive and boring.

✓ From your list of five people you're praying for that they'll become Christians. Write their names on a card or paper and put it in your pocket during the day. This is your IMPACT list. Whenever you remember the list throughout the day, pray for them! In your mind, and in the terminology of your prayers—put them in God's Funnel, and lay a Siege of Love around them!

Notes and Next Steps

Healthy Living

Chapter Eleven

There was a time when I thought I would probably be the last person to write anything intelligent—and personally tested—about healthy living! I suppose I might have qualified if we considered how many times I attempted to change to live a healthy lifestyle of good nutrition and exercise—and failed.

As with all of the other areas of life where it is possible to drift into the path of least resistance, maintaining healthy living only happens when we are doing so intentionally—by no-default living.

First of all, here are my confessions. I am a work-in-progress and my own healthy living choices are reasonably recent. In addition, I know little about the detailed sciences of health, nutrition, or fitness. The things I do know are not university-level material; at best, they are basic and very practical.

My definition of healthy living is very basic and specific: I am only talking about good nutrition and physical fitness. I realize there are so many other things that could be discussed when someone mentions healthy living!

And finally the clarification: this is not a diet, nutrition, and fitness manual. In this chapter, there are no nutritional information labels to read, no exercise diagrams to use, and no favourite recipes to try.

As I reference my own journey, I'm going to curb my temptation to write everything I think I've learned about the topic of healthy living. Instead, I'll explain my own process. There are already excellent source materials available on all of the related topics; find the ones that appeal to you, and use them.

Default Health

In telling my own story of moving away from the default lifestyle I drifted into, I hope to encourage you to make an intentional change in your lifestyle too!

I always gave an approving nod to the ideas of healthy living—but lived a no-default life following the path of least resistance. I enjoyed sports, was reasonably athletic growing up, but didn't make fitness a regular component of my life throughout university and beyond. I continually ate the wrong things! I didn't learn proper nutrition, nor was it modeled at home. Money was always a limiting factor, and good food always seemed more expensive! My life became busy and pressure filled. The easiest thing to eliminate from my hectic schedule seemed to be regular exercise! (You've heard of the tyranny of the urgent? Urgent things in your schedule are rarely the really important things!) Comfort food was a big part of my life! All these things resulted in me becoming overweight, feeling tired, and generally unhealthy. When I changed my life insurance carrier, I had to have a medical examination. The insurance company charged me 50% more than the standard rate because of my extra weight!

There are times when I feel like a regular attender at AA meetings who has fallen off the wagon too many times. Our comparison here is actually quite appropriate. Culturally, we tend to look down on people who suffer from alcohol or substance abuse; yet, on the other hand, so many of us are obese or terribly unhealthy for similar reasons to substance abusers! The difference is that for some of us our particular addictions and abuses revolve around food rather than alcohol or drugs!

The main point of consideration revolves around the why of unhealthy lifestyle choices. Why do our choices (or more accurately, lack of them) always cause us to drift toward living by default, toward just letting life happen?! Could it be that we allow ourselves to drift into a lifestyle of poor eating and little exercise because we don't value ourselves properly? It's not that we don't know what's best for us; we just don't do it! Are we simply too lazy to care? Although personal laziness can certainly be our favoured explanation for our lack of appropriate lifestyle choices, I think the idea of not valuing ourselves properly resonates with our common experience.

No-Default Health

A no-default approach to healthy living, then, is one in which we declare to ourselves "My life is valuable and worth treasuring!" If I truly believe that, then I will make the effort required for significant health improvements.

I began to apply a no-default approach to my health. I began to be intentional about my choices regarding food and exercise, just as I am in my marriage, my prayer life, and my finances. The success and freedom I've found by applying a no-default approach in these areas of my life really encouraged me to take a similar approach to my health and to expect success. I set goals, I made a plan, and I made myself accountable to others.

My Simple, Five Point Plan

Compose a wellness vision for my no-default healthy living choices.

1. Set goals.

2. Equip myself with knowledge.

3. Improve my self-talk, and change my perspective through declarative no-default statements.

4. Get an accountability partner.

My Simple, Five Point Plan Expanded

1. Vision

This is my vision for myself: I am strong, healthy, vibrant, and I pursue physical challenges!

This vision is the compelling force behind all the goals I have set for myself.

2. Goals

I set myself what G.T. Doran calls SMART goals. SMART goals are:

- specific

- measurable

- action-based

- reasonable

- time-oriented

Using these parameters for goal setting allows me to set goals which are achievable and which will give me measurable success. The idea is that as I am successful I will be encouraged to set more goals and achieve more success!

These are my nutrition and fitness goals for the first six months of this year:

- I will enter a 5 km race

- I will lose 25 lbs

- I will invest forty-five minutes in weight training, three times a week

- I will invest thirty minutes in walking and jogging, three times a week

- I will eliminate breads and sugar products from my diet

- I will include fruits and vegetables in my everyday diet

- I will sleep at least seven hours per night

3. Knowledge

Even a small amount of knowledge can motivate huge life changes.

I've been learning about nutrition. Please understand that I am not an expert.

Even if I communicated everything I know about nutrition, this would still be a very short chapter! So let's proceed this way: I'll share with you the information that surprised me and moved me toward taking responsibility for healthy choices and being intentional about nutrition and fitness.

Much of the biology of weight gain relates to blood sugar levels in the blood stream. When foods are high in sugars (or some form of carbohydrate that can be quickly converted into simple sugars), the body experiences a blood-sugar spike. The sugar level must be regulated by the brain and kept within a specific range, so insulin is used to reduce the sugar concentration in the blood by converting it into glycogen. Glycogen is easily stored and accumulated (when not used) as body fat.

I had a diet filled with sugars, breads, and potatoes. I discovered these foods easily break down into simple sugars! Take bread for example: it is a simple carbohydrate that the body very quickly breaks down into sugar! Potatoes are even worse! These types of foods that have a quick impact on increasing the blood's sugar level are called high glycemic foods.

Problems ensue as our blood sugar control systems are stressed to the limit by these high glycemic foods. In some cases, the overwhelming sugar levels push the pancreas to produce more and more insulin until our cells become actually resistant to insulin. This inability of the body to properly manage the insulin and sugar concentrations coupled with insulin resistance is called metabolic disorder and can lead to diabetes.

Cutting the refined sugars, wheat products, and potatoes from my diet was a huge step forward toward health and wellness!

My limited knowledge of nutrition together with my experiences and observations were enough to motivate me to take responsibility for my own health and move into my preferred future!

4. Self Talk

Using declarative, no-default statements I can verbalize and rehearse multiple times daily works really well for me. I make my declarative statements frequently. For example, I have them on the bathroom mirror, by the front door, in my car and lots of other places. I repeat them whenever I see them.

These statements make me think better by changing my perspective and reinforcing my goals; they help me feel better by verbalizing what is true at times when my resolve is slipping.

These are my nutrition and fitness no-default

statements:

- I am healthy, strong, and vibrant.

- My choices are the pathways to my preferred future.

- My choices don't limit me, they empower me to reach my goals.

- I am valuable to God and others!

- God's favour brings me the benefits of right choices!

5. Accountability

As I've said so many times in this book, having an accountability partner is an essential part of living a no-default life. My wife, Carrie, is my nutrition and fitness accountability partner. Everything about our accountability arrangement is to reinforce the goals I have set.

Carrie knows that, as my accountability partner, she needs to:

- Be an encourager, not a critic.

- Be both goal-oriented and gracious.

- Be in frequent contact.

- Be able to anticipate the challenges ahead.

- Be willing to rehearse my no-default statements with me.

This part of my no-default lifestyle is a work-in-progress. I believe that by being intentional about my health I will discover the same freedom, joy, and abundant life I've found when I've refused to live by default in other areas of my life.

What Can You Do Right Now to Adopt a Healthy, No-Default Lifestyle?

- ✓ Reflect on past health choices, specifically nutrition and exercise. Do your past choices reflect what you really believe about your true value? Remember, God was willing to pay the price of His Son's life to ransom you. You are precious in His sight!

- ✓ Write down a statement about your worth and value in God's eyes.

- ✓ Write your own wellness vision statement.

- ✓ Using my example from the chapter as a template, compose your own five point plan, including your own list of declarative no-default statements.

Notes and Next Steps

Conclusion

We have briefly examined eleven areas:

1. Your Identity
2. The Calling On Your Life
3. Responsibility vs. Self-Reliance
4. Forgiveness
5. Spiritual Warfare
6. Facing Your Fears
7. The Power of the Secret Life
8. Finances
9. Marriage
10. Prayer
11. Health

In each of these areas, the Lord has brought huge and lasting changes into my life because I was no longer willing to live by default, by thinking, "Oh, things will just work out". The truth is, things don't ever just work out!

You might think, "Well, I didn't worry much about it, and my life seems to have worked out okay." We can all be blinded by our mediocre expectations of life; I was! But Jesus didn't plan for us to live mediocre, "okay" lives. He describes the life his planned for us as *abundant* (John 10:10)!

Taking responsibility for your life and choices, earnestly seeking, honestly questioning, and intentionally deciding to live a no-default life is the only way to have what the Lord promised us in Jeremiah 29:11:

> *For I know the plans I have for you, says the Lord. They are plans for good and not for disaster, to give you a future and a hope. In those days when you pray, I will listen. If you look for Me in earnest [with all your heart], you will find Me when you seek Me. I will be found by you, says the Lord.*

Aren't you happy that the Lord doesn't approach your relationship with Him by default, just letting it happen randomly? As this verse in Jeremiah makes so clear—Jesus has plans for you! And they're plans with a future and a hope—plans to bring good into your life!

The Lord Himself is a no-default God! He has plans and a purpose that started before the world was formed. That's why we're told Jesus was seen in the book of Revelation, as *"a Lamb who was slaughtered before the world was made"* (13:8).

How is that possible? Jesus was crucified at a specific time in history, just over 2000 years ago! The death of Jesus on the cross, like a sacrificial lamb slain, was part of the plan—it had already been accomplished in the mind and heart of God.

My prayer is that the contents of this book will spur you on to examine the different areas of your life, determine where you are living by-default, and take steps to live intentionally towards the future God has planned for you!

About Jim Gordon

Jim and his wife, Carrie, founded the-intimate-couple.com in 2007, and have written seven ebooks, including the *7-Day Sex Challenge*, and *99 Questions to Ask Before Saying, 'I Do!'* The-intimate-couple.com is dedicated to assisting couples obtain the kind of marriage God designed—the marriage of their dreams!

In addition, Jim writes at jimgordon.ca with leaders in mind. This site is devoted to equipping those who want to increase their capacity for influence and become architects of culture and change. His encouragement is to move into God's preferred future—all within the context of the message of grace!

Jim and Carrie live in Ontario, Canada and have nine children and eight grandchildren who are best described as *awesome*!

Jim is Lead Pastor of the Elora Road Christian Fellowship.

JimGordon.ca

41236393R00084

Made in the USA
Charleston, SC
26 April 2015